the beach

a celebration of life

SWEETWATER
PRESS

SWEETWATER
PRESS

The Beach

Produced by arrangement with Sweetwater Press

ISBN-13: 978-1-58173-648-9
ISBN-10: 1-58173-648-7

Book and text by Patrick Covert
Printed in China

the beach

Words cannot adequately describe the beach because it has so many faces. Nothing quite calms the soul like the gentle crash of ocean waves that venture deeper into the mind than anything man has ever been able to produce. But when it takes a notion to rise up in anger there is nothing that can stop it or dampen its wrath.

The beach, in its many incarnations, has the power to offer up every emotion known to mankind and a few yet to be explained. The spectrum of feelings, from peace and serenity to excitement and fear, are played out simultaneously through the world every day on its shores in symphonic portions meant for humans to enjoy, respect, and learn from.

There are over 221,000 miles of coastline on the planet earth, each mile telling a story of its own. Some of the finest are featured here.

Holland coast

Florida pavers

Koh Larn Island, Thailand

Costa Rica

There are
places
beyond our
wildest
dreams,
where
palm trees
rise
out of
nowhere
amid
sugary
sands and
wild blue
yonder.

Kirsiu Nerija National Park, Lithuania

Kirsiu Nerija National Park, Lithuania

Jensen Beach, Florida

Pebble washing

Carmel, California

Clearwater, Florida

Fort Morgan, Alabama

Dillon Beach, California

Private stash

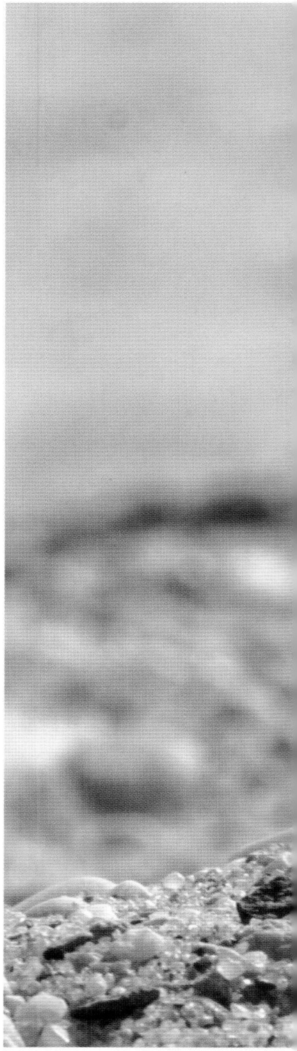

Previous page: Jupiter Beach, Florida

Buried treasure

Calais, France

A

morning

jog on

the beach,

alone

with

a friend,

makes for

moments

that will

run through

the mind

forever.

Mullet rush

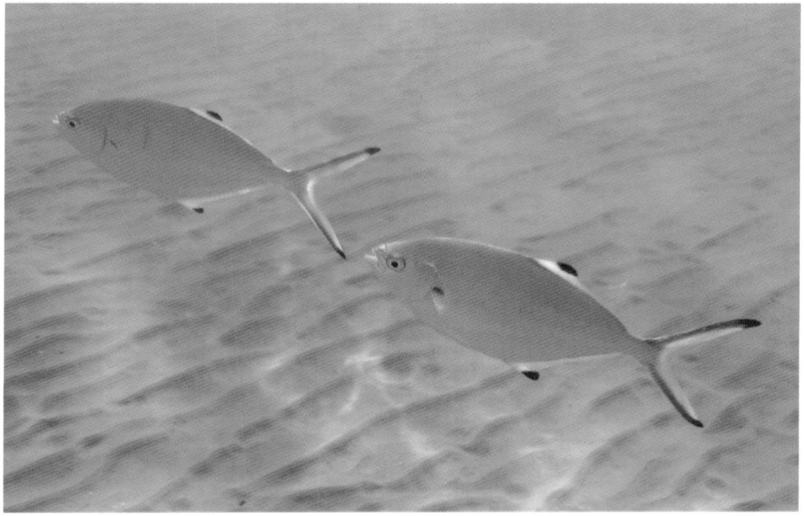

Zakynthos, Greece

Previous page: Sea of Cortez, Mexico

Florida

Morning Glories, Australia

Gulf of Mexico

Island of Fehmarn, Germany

Little Talbot Island State Park, Florida

Hilton Head Island, South Carolina

Tahahoma, New Zealand

Spot color sunny day

Caribbean

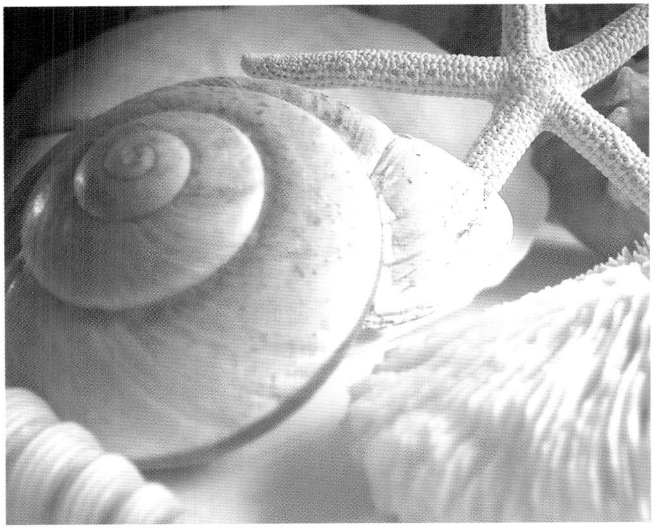

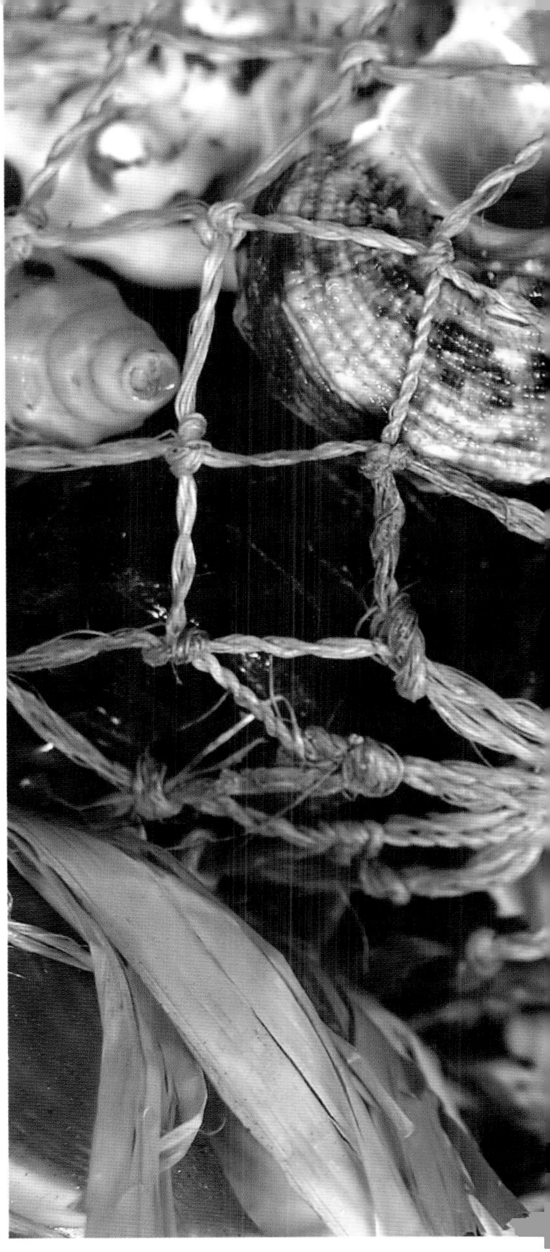

Previous page: Aitutaki Lagoon, Cook Islands

Iridescent snail

Chesapeake Bay, Virginia

St. Augustine, Florida

Just a

short walk

on the

beach

is all

it takes

to forget

all that

is made

of anything

other

than sand

or water.

Sierra Leone, West Africa

Having it all to yourself

Tybee Island, Georgia

Bahamas

Gulf Shores, Alabama

White on white

Palm Beach, Florida

An afternoon break

Rangiora, Tahiti

At times

the beach

is meant

to be

shared

from the

perspective

of two.

Koh Larn Island, Pattaya, Thailand

At anchor on a summer's day

Previous page: Tobago Cays, St. Vincent, Grenadines

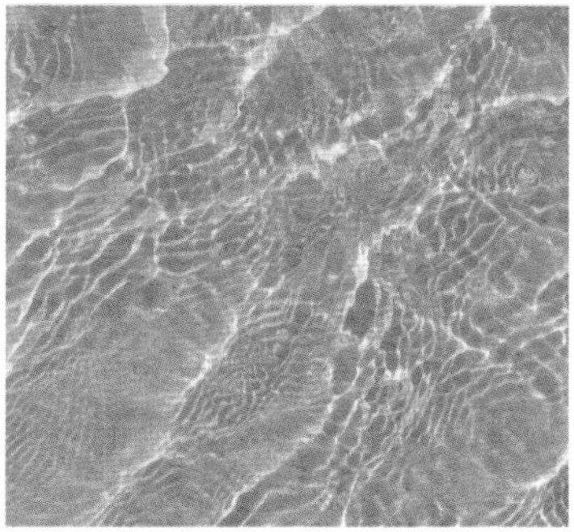

Gold is

sometimes

more precious

in its

unladen form,

a mass

lighter than air

that can only

be captured

in the camera

of the mind.

Antigua

An old timer

Sculptured serenity

St. Thomas, US Virgin Islands

And the tide rushes in

Fort Morgan, Alabama

Curling waveforms

The sun

plays games

with the

shadows,

particularly

late, just

before

leaving work

for the day.

North Carolina

There's something

about the beach

you can't put your

finger on.

Or maybe

there are

too many things

to put your

finger on.

Mediterranean Sea

Cantabrico Sea

Sand patterns

Shell series #1

Shell series #2

Whitehaven Island, Australia

Cape Hatteras, North Carolina

Rush of tide

Birds seem

to enjoy

the beach,

although

they do

have their

moments.

Duck, North Carolina

Pembrokeshire coast, Wales

Sanibel Island, Florida

Glassine blue afternoon

The blue

world

of the dolphin

reflects

the freedom

birds find

in the sky

above.

Bottlenose dolphin

Gliders

Clear day soaring

Caribbean

North Shore, Hawaii

Acapulco, Mexico

Pembrokeshire coast, Wales

Naples Beach, Florida

Not all

of life is

perfection.

The beauty

in life is

finding

the perfect

in the

imperfect.

The last stop

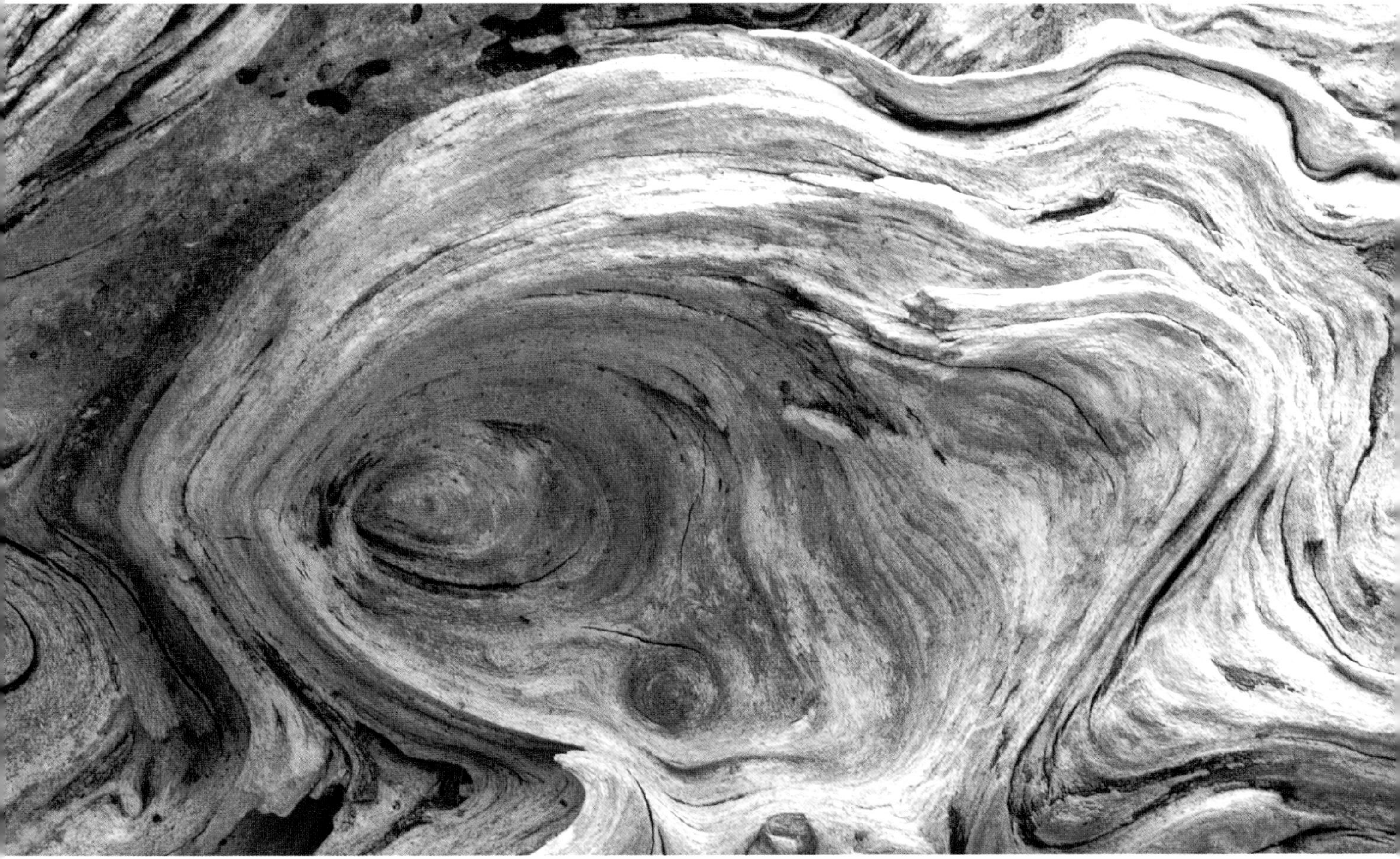

Nature's never-ending sculpture

Atlantic Ocean

Previous page: Baltic Sea

Cook Islands

Costa Rica

Calanques beach, Marseille, France

Netherlands

Outer Banks, North Carolina

We are

not the

only

living

creatures

who

seem to

enjoy

the

beach.

Green on white

Barbados

Serenity

is often

found

in an

atmosphere

where time

is of

little

importance.

Lanikai Beach, Hawaii

To have

the dunes

to one's self

is to hold

the world

captive

in selfish

awe.

Cape Cod, Massachusetts

South Padre Island, Texas

Malibu Beach, California

Pembrokeshire coast, Wales

Turquoise

is

never more

brilliant

than when

found

on the

ocean's

floor.

Beer Beach, United Kingdom

Rockaway Beach, Oregon

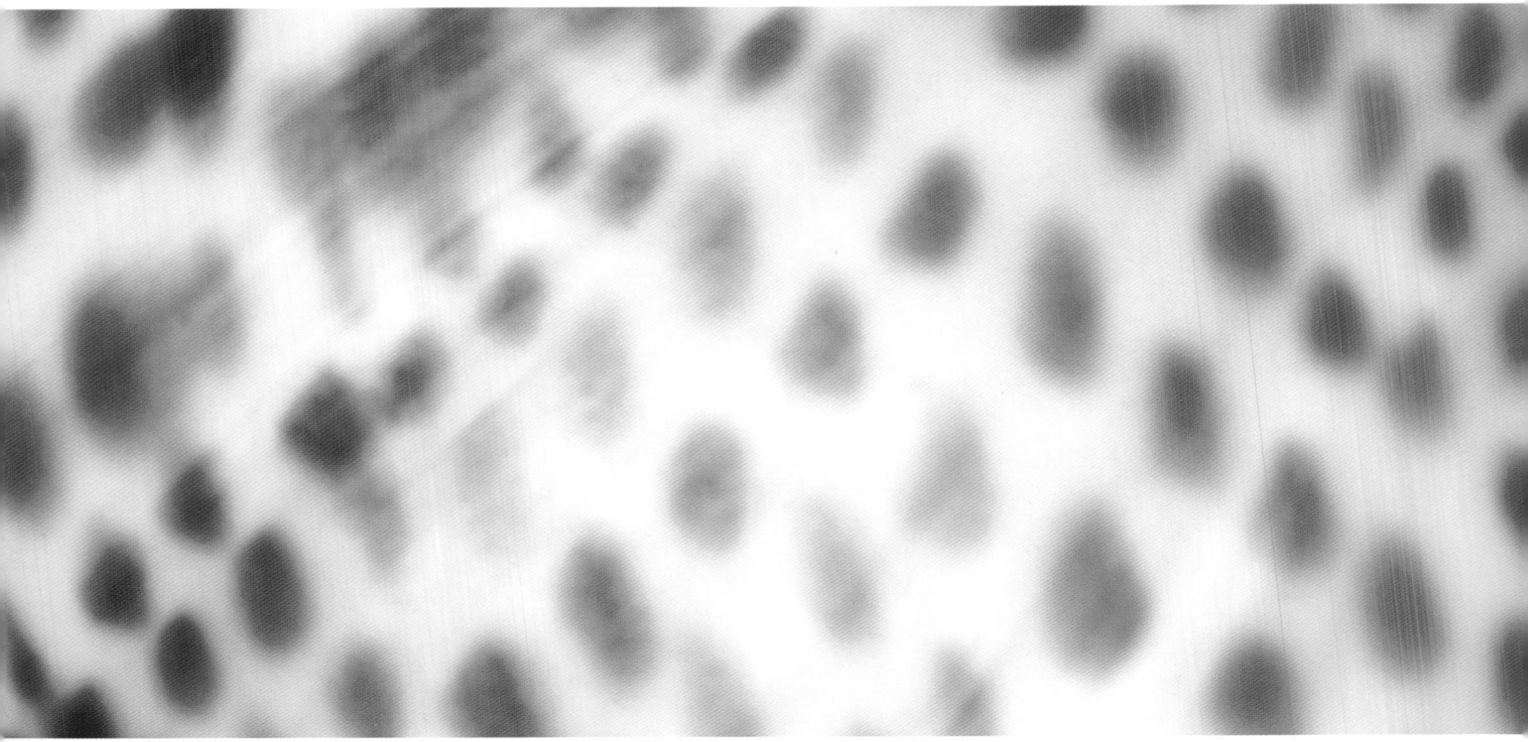

Sea snail

Coast of Germany, Baltic Sea

El Matador Beach, Malibu, California

Previous page: Jobson's Cove, Bermuda

The Seychelles

Bora Bora

Cozumel, Mexico

Belize

Cumberland Island, Georgia

The wind

dancing

through

the grass

is a daily

performance

worth

catching.

Clearwater, Florida

Manisota Key, Florida

Windward Point Bay, Anguilla

Spanish Lookout Caye, Belize

Joy

Sand Dollar Beach, Big Sur, California